D1707926

AMERICAN QUARTER HORSES

by Amanda Parise-Peterson

CAPSTONE PRESS
a capstone imprint

Snap Books are published by Capstone Press,
1710 Roe Crest Drive, North Mankato, Minnesota 56003
www.mycapstone.com

Library of Congress Cataloging-in-Publication Data
Library of Congress Cataloging-in-Publication Data is available
on the Library of Congress website.
ISBN: 978-1-5435-0032-5 (hardcover)
ISBN: 978-1-5435-0038-7 (paperback)
ISBN: 978-1-5435-0044-8 (eBook PDF)

Editorial Credits
Amy Kortuem, editor
Kayla Rossow, designer
Morgan Walters, media researcher
Kathy McColley, production specialist

Image Credits
Alamy: Jim Lane, 27, Niday Picture Library, 6; Getty Images: Alex Grimm,
26; Shutterstock: blue67design, (floral sketch) design element throughout,
Candia Baxter, 24, Creative Travel Projects, 2, 3, jacotakepics, 8, Jana
Mackova, 14, 15, Juliata, (floral) design element throughout, Julie
Vader, 23, Kobby Dagan, 16, 17, 18, 20, L. Kramer, (fish scale) design
throughout, Lenkadan, Cover, 11, 13, Maros Bauer, 29, Pavlo Burdyak, 4,
redstone, (paper background) design element throughout, suns07butterfly,
(watercolor) design element throughout, Todd Klassy, 12, Vera Zinkova, 5,
yod67, (horse vector) design element, Zuzule, 1; Wikimedia: J. C. Buttre, 9

Printed and bound in the USA.
010779S18

TABLE OF CONTENTS

CHAPTER 1

Calm Companions

People sometimes call the American Quarter Horse the golden retriever of the horse world. Like golden retriever dogs, Quarter Horses are calm, loyal, and cooperative.

Quarter Horses do well in many areas. They herd cattle on ranches and perform at rodeos. People also use Quarter Horses for trail riding, racing, and shows.

American Quarter Horses are prized for their strength and gentleness.

AMERICAN HORSES

Before 1519 no horses lived in North America. That year Spanish explorer Hernán Cortés brought horses to Mexico. The European explorers and settlers who followed Cortés also brought horses.

Settlers traded horses to American Indians. Trading helped the horses spread to what is now Texas, New Mexico, and California.

In the late 1800s cowboys used Quarter Horses for ranch work.

BREEDING

In the 1600s and 1700s English settlers brought **Hobby** and **Thoroughbred** horses to North America. People bred the sleek Thoroughbreds and muscular Hobbies to North American horses. The offspring were the first American Quarter Horses.

Quarter Horses quickly became popular with settlers. The smart, sturdy horses herded cattle, provided transportation, and helped clear land for farms. They also ran fast. Many of them won quarter-mile (.4-kilometer) races. Quarter Horses were named after this distance.

Hobby—a small horse breed that began in Ireland
Thoroughbred—a breed of horse raised for racing

OFFICIAL BREED

In 1940 the American Quarter Horse became an official horse breed. That year several Quarter Horse owners formed the American Quarter Horse Association (AQHA) in Amarillo, Texas. The AQHA started a registry for Quarter Horse breeding records.

Today Quarter Horses are the most popular horses in the world with the largest breed registry. More than 5.5 million horses are registered with the AQHA, which serves about 350,000 members around the world.

Sir Archy

Important Ancestors

Some Quarter Horse **ancestors** played a key role in the development of the breed. A chestnut horse named Janus was born in England in 1746. Ten years later, his owner brought him to the Virginia colony in North America.

Janus looked different from other horses at the time. He was large-boned and compact. His muscular back legs helped him run fast. Janus passed on his qualities to his **foals**.

Sir Archy and Shiloh were also important to the Quarter Horse breed. Sir Archy was a champion racehorse who sired at least 300 champion foals. One of his descendants, Shiloh, became a famous racehorse in Texas.

In the 1850s people called Steel Dust the fastest horse in Texas. He was so popular that many people called early Quarter Horses "Steel Dusts."

ancestor–a member of a breed that lived a long time ago
foal–a horse that is less than 1 year old

9

Chapter 2

America's Workhorse

Quarter Horses have large, muscular body frames. Their firm, strong bodies give Quarter Horses a straight stride. Their build also helps them move quickly and lightly.

Strong hindquarters give Quarter Horses their speed. The muscular hindquarters thrust them forward from standing into a fast run.

Quarter Horses have short, wide heads. Their ears are small. The eyes are large and alert. Quarter Horses have large nostrils. Their nostrils help them breathe quickly and deeply while running.

FACT
The American Quarter Horse is the state horse of Texas. The breed played an important role in the history of the state.

American Quarter Horses
are large and muscular.

A Colorful Breed

Quarter Horses can be one of 16 color patterns. The most common color is **sorrel**, which is red-brown. Other common colors are black, chestnut, brown, and gray. Chestnut horses are a shade of copper or red. Dun, buckskin, and red dun are all shades of brown.

a palomino Quarter Horse (front)

sorrel—a red-brown color

Quarter Horses can be bay, palomino, or grullo. Bay horses range from deep tan to dark brown-red. They have black manes, tails, and lower legs. A palomino is tan with a lighter mane and tail. Grullos are gray. Their manes and tails are black, and their heads are dark brown or black.

Roan is another color pattern found in Quarter Horses. Roan horses have white hairs mixed with hair of a darker color.

Cremello and perlino are less common color patterns. Both cremellos and perlinos have pink skin, white or cream-colored coats, and blue eyes.

CALM AND QUIET

Quarter Horses are known for their cooperative personalities. They are calm and gentle. They work hard to please their owners.

Quarter Horses are willing and able to do many jobs. They herd cattle, pull carts and wagons, and carry riders on their backs.

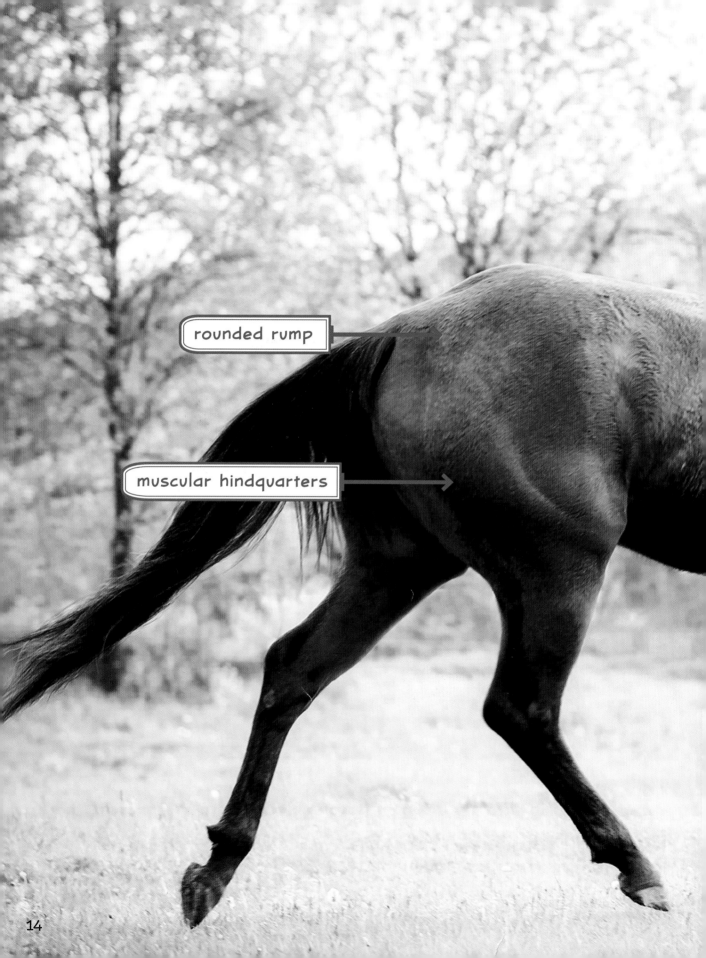

rounded rump

muscular hindquarters

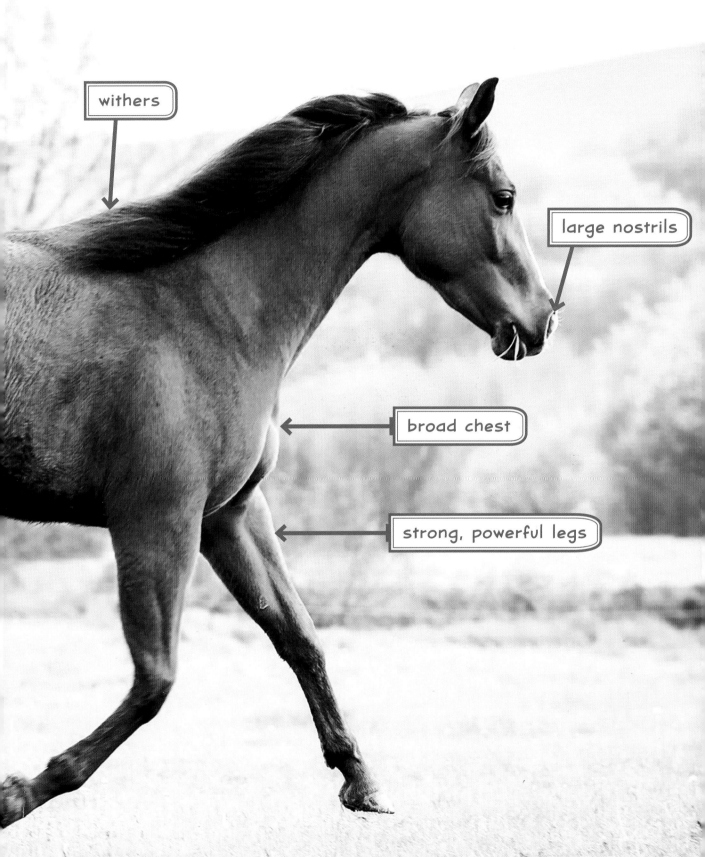

withers

large nostrils

broad chest

strong, powerful legs

CHAPTER 3

Stars of the Rodeo

People still race Quarter Horses and use them to herd cattle. Many Quarter Horses also compete in **rodeos**. Rodeo events test the skills of horses and riders. The events require teamwork and speed.

RODEOS

Beginning in the mid-1800s cowboys made money by rounding up huge herds of roaming cattle. For fun the cowboys held contests in roping cattle and other ranch skills. People started calling the contests rodeos. Quarter Horses became one of the most popular breeds to use in rodeos.

rodeo—a competition in which people ride horses and bulls and rope cattle

Some rodeo events test the horse's ability to work with cattle.

RODEO EVENTS

Today's rodeos include both herding and nonherding events. Competitors spend a lot of time practicing for each event.

Riders try not to knock down barrels as they race.

In barrel races three barrels are set up in the arena in the pattern of a triangle. Horses race in a cloverleaf pattern around the barrels. The best barrel racing runs take only about 17 seconds. Judges add 5 seconds for each barrel knocked to the ground.

In most rodeo events the fastest time wins. But in saddle bronc and bareback riding the longest time wins. The rider must stay on the bucking horse for a certain number of seconds.

Horses chase a calf or **steer** during roping events. In tie-down roping events, the rider gets off the horse and ties the cow's legs together. In dally team roping, another rider throws a rope around the cow's back legs. Both riders wrap the ropes twice around the saddle horns. The horses then quickly stop and pull back on the ropes to keep the animal under control.

FACT

Quarter Horses are said to have "cow sense," or a natural ability to work with cattle. They are able to predict the movement of cattle before their riders can. Western ranchers formed the first Quarter Horse association to protect this special sense when breeding.

steer—a young male bull

Well-trained Quarter Horses match their speed to the cattle's speed. The horses make quick changes in direction. The rider can then focus on roping the calf or steer.

In steer wrestling rodeo events, riders get off their horses to bring a steer to the ground.

TEAMWORK

Training for rodeos takes time and practice. Riders and their Quarter Horses must learn to work as a team. The horses should respond quickly to commands from their riders. Riders use their legs, reins, body positions, and voices to give signals to the horses.

Some Quarter Horses are better suited for certain events. For example, not all Quarter Horses make good barrel racing horses. They must be quick and have excellent balance to race around the barrels.

PRCA

The Professional Rodeo Cowboys Association (PRCA) is the largest and oldest rodeo organization in the world. Each year, the PRCA sanctions about 600 rodeo events in the United States and Canada, awarding prize money to the winners. The PRCA also raises money for charities. In December the top riders end the season with the National Finals Rodeo in Las Vegas, Nevada.

Chapter 4

Quarter Horses in Action

Quarter Horses are still used to herd cattle on ranches. Many Quarter Horses race or compete in horse shows. Quarter Horses also are good choices for trail riding and other pleasure riding.

Quarter Horse Shows

The American Quarter Horse Association sponsors many horse shows in the United States each year. Each November the AQHA holds the World Championship Show. The show lasts for 15 days and awards a total of about $2.3 million in money and other prizes to the winners.

American Quarter Horses make excellent pleasure riding horses.

In Western events riders usually wear a cowboy hat and a long-sleeved shirt.

WESTERN PERFORMANCE

Western performance competitions include horse show and rodeo events. Western pleasure and horsemanship are show events. Rodeo events include **reining** and team penning.

In Western pleasure events riders guide their horses at a slow pace around the show ring. The horses walk, jog, and lope. Judges score them on appearance and ability. In horsemanship events judges rate the rider's abilities.

REINING AND PENNING

Team penning is a fast-growing Western performance event in the United States. Three riders rely on their horses' "cow sense" to separate three marked cattle from a herd. The riders gather the marked cattle into a pen.

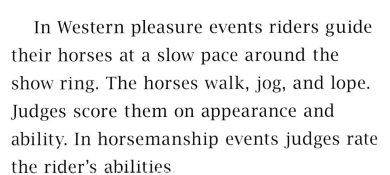

reining—an event where riders guide their horses through spins, sliding stops, and other exercises

In reining events riders guide their horses through exercises such as spins and sliding stops. During sliding stops horses run at full speed. They dig their back feet into the ground and slide to a stop.

In reining events a horse slides to a stop at its rider's command.

RACING

The quarter-mile is still the most popular distance for Quarter Horses to race. Top Quarter Horses run a quarter-mile in about 21 seconds. They reach speeds of 55 miles (89 km) per hour.

Quarter-mile races are held at racetracks all over North America. Many races also take place at state and county fairs.

The American Quarter Horse has been prized for years for its gentle personality and hardworking nature. This "golden retriever" of the horse world will keep winning new fans and friends in the future.

Quarter Horses speed down a racetrack in Lexington, Kentucky.

Fast Facts:
The American Quarter Horse

Name: American Quarter Horses get their name from quarter-mile races.

History: The breed began in North America in the 1700s. The American Quarter Horse became an official breed in 1940.

Height: Quarter Horses are 15 or 16 hands (about 5 feet or 1.5 meters) tall at the withers. Each hand equals 4 inches (10 centimeters).

Weight: 1,200 to 1,500 pounds (540 to 680 kilograms)

Colors: Quarter Horses can be one of 16 color patterns. Common colors are sorrel, chestnut, bay, black, brown, gray, and roan.

Features: muscular hindquarters; long legs; short, broad head; small muzzle; large nostrils

Personality: calm, cooperative, gentle

Abilities: Quarter Horses are excellent all-around horses. They are the most common horses used for ranch work and rodeos. They are also good choices for trail riding, racing, and shows.

Life span: 20 to 30 years

Glossary

ancestor (AN-sess-tur)—a member of a breed that lived a long time ago

foal (FOHL)—a horse that is less than 1 year old

Hobby (HAW-bee)—a small horse breed that began in Ireland

lope (LOHP)—a three-beat gait of a horse that is slower than a gallop

reining (RAYN-ing)—an event where riders guide their horses through spins, sliding stops, and other exercises

rodeo (ROH-dee-oh)—a competition in which people ride horses and bulls and rope cattle

sanction (SANGK-shun)—to officially approve or support

sorrel (SOR-uhl)—a red-brown color

steer (STEER)—a young male bull

Thoroughbred (THUHR-oh-bred)—a breed of horse raised for racing

Read More

Dell, Pamela. *American Quarter Horses.* Majestic Horses. North Mankato, Minn.: Child's World, Inc., 2014.

Kolpin, Molly. *Favorite Horses: Breeds Girls Love.* Crazy About Horses. North Mankato, Minn.: Capstone Press, 2015.

Graubart, Norman. *Horses in American History.* How Animals Shaped History. New York: PowerKids Press, 2015.

Internet Sites

Use FactHound to find Internet sites related to this book.

Visit *www.facthound.com*

Just type in 9781543500325 and go.

 Check out projects, games and lots more at **www.capstonekids.com**

InDex

DATE DUE

			PRINTED IN U.S.A.